TOTAL MEMORY

poems by

STEPHANIE ADAMS-SANTOS

Finishing Line Press
Georgetown, Kentucky

TOTAL MEMORY

Copyright © 2016 by Stephanie Adams-Santos
ISBN 978-1-63534-030-3 First Edition
All rights reserved under International and Pan-American Copyright Conventions.
No part of this book may be reproduced in any manner whatsoever without written permission from the publisher, except in the case of brief quotations embodied in critical articles and reviews.

ACKNOWLEDGMENTS

Publisher: Leah Maines

Editor: Christen Kincaid

Cover Art: Stephanie Adams-Santos

Author Photo: Robin Sola

Cover Design: Stephanie Adams-Santos

Printed in the USA on acid-free paper.
Order online: www.finishinglinepress.com
        also available on amazon.com

                Author inquiries and mail orders:
                      Finishing Line Press
                      P. O. Box 1626
                Georgetown, Kentucky 40324
                        U. S. A.

The brief span of an individual life is misleading. Each one of us is as old as the entire biological kingdom, & our bloodstreams are tributaries of the great sea of its total memory.

– **J.G. Ballard**, *The Drowned World*

*

I slip out for an hour alone—

*

I slip into aloneness
as into a silk shift

—I have slipped into myself

    —am in the living diary
              of blood, now

*

Alone
in the black fern walls

of my interior:
    its shadows

& gymnosperms shine
with the eyes opening

they are opening

      soft & green

  mad & green

*

The door is splitting with darkness

what is beating?

I follow
 into a hollow into a graze
of hollowing, I graze
 on the drum sound:

waterwater
against the boards

 the boards splitting with darkness
bahhp   bahhp   bahhp

 Now—the hallucinations
(the little vision-burns of all these years)
can come, come up to the surface
 of the brain:

fins, bodies, fish, fish, blood of fish
darkens every flesh I have

*

a wet thud hitting like

    bahhp bahhpbahhp

I thrash
         I sleep
                  I thrash

I thrash like a—

    (through this Silence)

        this, this, this
        the monsoon of time

bahhp bahhpbahhp
go the fins in my memory

            moving me along

*

I hold me inside
                              & turn it in my fingers
                              to no end,

    turn again a prism

but for what kind of spectrum?
                              Inside the body is no light

—beneath this shimmering skim
                                        are clouds

suspended in murk, precognitive

      as agate, a wise color for eyes

                (some wise eyes have
                the savvy of sunk flesh)

*

    Mother-of-Pearl,

eye & eye & eye & eye
                amid the sediment

        unfocused, blank
   with vortex

*

                        I lean in
        to the mirror

to the white mask of the water

to the sensate clamshell edge
fidgeting with lashes

—in her eyes,

        in her dug-out, half-
imagined holes

        I can see me dreaming

*

I am deep inside

deep past even myself

deeply myself

this is a prayer
       this edge

this is the site
of prayer, this greenblack
mirror where I gaze

       to you
       to your eyes, queer
            creature in me

how old are you—
         leaping out so many legs?

*

Have I fallen away?

A whorl in the pond

*

bahhp   bahhp   bahhp

Something burns a symbol
                     in my ears, a poem

   I cannot reach though I can let
wound me:

an ocarina playing notes
in the shape of an egg, below
          where your gills are waving & serene

*

I want so much

I want to enter it I want
  to dehisce in wind
in water like you do

in wind & in water:
  to shatter the thin silk of a slip

to blow it in the coarse element, multiply
  & bury

its seeds in the big blind eyes
of saturniids

*

What is it to fly into burning?

Before silence spits me out
of this hole

                will something other
                    tell me

will you, who are pronounced as bone, uneven
mother-of-pearl & sleepy

in the
mouth-headed bowl of the sea, tell me

        will I

will I
                will I

*

      Will these big moth wings
clamber out & eclipse

           overtake
this suffering?

                O yes
O yes

      but first—

*

Something

something
is threading a wet cord
through the nose
     & pulls

so I go sloshing with
the scent of blood
with animal temper with
red
discord, hoping for more
(more body)
    & want sleep—

*

So here

no lush sound
rests

& here in the past the hands of apes & newts
closed in unison
       around the same emptiness

Here shutter out the light
in my palm

  like that

now the blades of grass are lifted in me
(once again) like the buffalo's meal,

quietly touching

      at the roots

*

Mothering fish, fern, shook
casket of boughs

      what burns in my skull

I think a poem still nascent
with primordial flesh

I think an egg brooding in the shape of music

*

Do you, in your red door
admit me?

                in your green door unfit me

*

(the hope is to arrive
amid the door-high ferns
& come open

to leave skin at the architrave,
to be so exceeded—

        as a locust, a viper, wind
                sloughed off a lyre)

*

Do you?

in the ticking of the mind-clock
make a soundless second stroke in me, won't you
fill my corpus with a sigh &

let me sleep
into the total memory of earth?

*

    & what beyond?

It is an egg I see inside/out—

An imminence with organs

                This pulsing eye
        whose soft shell breathes

(the stars)

*

I lean
& suck at the whorls—

   There are so many others I sense
clustered in the near fields
watching

      Only their crystal-eyes
    can truly say

what portion of me is clasped
in the great serpent's hand

(the stars)

*

I hear the mute soft cinders
sifting in my hair

Who can say

where the agate axe cuts down
old sounds
into corymbs of ash

                Open your hands—

I sleep

(& where the old self
splits her head
on a purple inflorescence

        is my hallowed history
        alert)

*

Now the soft stars' mouths
fasten to my brain

who can say

        who can say

now again the blades of grass are lifting in me

        they are lifting in my greenness
when the far light shoots down
swimming to the seed—

    This is memory

*

Touch my tongue

Unpack, un-parse this melody,
                             a memory

              this teeming recollection, fission like a star—

This stream on dark devours,
      crawls bellywise without
                    a head & I drown

to tread the shadows that have sunk

*

None can say

    where light folds in the ferns

  & escapes

But with my drowned mouth open

  I recall a thing

*

I slip out, I slip out—

    water, water in the dark
    & water's heat

An hour tunnels to the floor

I breathe so deep when I sleep

Stephanie Adams-Santos is a Guatemalan-American writer, educator, and tarot reader from Portland, Oregon. She is the author of *Swarm Queen's Crown* (Fathom Books, 2016) and several chapbooks—*Little Fugues* (Sola Books, 2015) and *The Sundering* (Poetry Society of America, 2009), which was selected by Linda Gregg as winner of the New York Chapbook Fellowship. Adams-Santos' poems have appeared in many print and online journals and magazines, including *Guernica Magazine, The Boston Review,* and *Orion*.